Nightscapes from Afar
A Collection

Tomasz Tatum

Nightscapes from Afar
A Collection

Bibliografische Information der Deutschen Nationalbibliothek:
Die Deutsche Nationalbibliothek verzeichnet diese Publikation in der Deutschen Nationalbibliografie; detaillierte bibliografische Daten sind im Internet über http://dnb.dnb.de abrufbar.

© USA 2015 T. Tatum *(www.tomasztatum.net)*

Cover Design and Illustration:
Designbüro Tina Dompert (www.tinadompert.de),
Images iStockphoto

Herstellung und Verlag: BoD – Books on Demand, Norderstedt

ISBN: 978-3-7431-9150-1

Contents

Foreword 1
National Youth 5
Evaporate! 6
Safe Keeping 7
Where'd Ya Think I was Going? 8
Heard It Yesterday 9
Back from LA 10
Injustice Every Day 12
A Puppet Life 14
Autumn 15
Futureworld 16
So Blue for Her 17
Blues from a Bottle 18
Bonefish Boogie 19
City Girl 20
Coming Up for Air 21
In December 22
Electrify Me 23
Hundred Years 24
Empty Houses 25
Falling Angels 26
Summer 27
Nighttime in America 28

Plenty of Reasons	30
Wanna Know Why	31
The It's-All-in-God's-Hands Blues	32
Hotspot	33
Rainy Days	34
An Invitation	35
Living your Lies	36
Online Tonight	37
Rambling with My Rohrschachs	38
Things You Do!	39
When the Americans Came	40
Riding the Bus	41
The Waiting Game	42
Spring and July	43
Taxi Blues	44
Sunset	45
Wanna be a Fan of Miley's	46
The Wind in your Face	47
Yer Beauty Mark	48
Lantern	49
In the Ocean	50
The Visit	51
Tricked Me into Thinking	52
Weekend Wager	53
You Told Me	54
Intercity	55

Foreword

Way back when I was a kid, one of my first real heroes was Dr. Seuss. From what I gather, his stories continue to sell well to this day, which I find fully justified and phenomenal, too. But I'm not sure whether this ongoing success is for the same reason as it was back then. Sure, the stories are funny and the characters populating his books are both sympathetic and zany. But, intentional or not, Dr. Seuss was teaching us something very significant as he stretched creative license to its limits with his rhymes and word concoctions. He taught us how to connect the dots not only linguistically but helped young readers see and recognize abstract notions while imparting values into his tales. Maybe I'm wrong, but I suspect that the *Grinch* or the *Cat in the Hat* are today mostly appreciated as good entertainment, simply because of their anarchic funniness. But it was his prose which, for me, was the first tentative step into a world which later grew, opening doors to progressively deeper fare.

While never averse to the prose and poetry which my schooling brought with it, I can't recall many of my teachers straying very far afield from standard fare: dead old men (and a few ladies). All was not lost upon a roomful of adolescents but Longfellow, Frost, Whitman and Dickenson resided on lofty pedestals, in part because of the indisputable craft and beauty of their work—but also because of the vast distance we juveniles felt toward the language and the themes of their work. They were the literary equivalents of alabaster busts of George Washington, important but with little in common with us. In high school, very few of us suspected something like a *McCarthyist* gap in American prose in the 20th century, but even fewer of us ever learned whether this was indeed so or why. Call it instinct, but we sensed a missing link, something residing between the otherworldliness of those early poets and what was later branded as pop culture.

Maybe it was Bob Dylan who changed this by rousing interest in the poetry and prose his music contained. And of the relevance it truly has in our perception of the world and of ourselves. At the end of the 1950s, American beat poets and writers were pushing the boundaries of prose and literature. And getting noticed. But, had I spent my adult life only in the US, I fear that I probably would have missed something. Later American work by writers like Ntozake Shange or Everette Maddox (which I discovered in German publications in the 1980s) didn't attract a lot of notice. Nor did mainstream America seem to care much about James Baldwin, Seamus Heaney or Rafael Alberti—at least not until they became Nobel Prize recipients or died.

I'm neither a critic nor a literature major, just someone who has spent a lot of time out there in the world, often in hotels and trains and planes. Or even, as the cliché goes, in cafés and bars. Taking the pulse of life around me while I did what I had to do to make a living. What follows is a selection of more than thirty years of trying to fathom what went on inside of me as my path crisscrossed those of others, a little like the African spirits hidden away in Amos Tutuola's *Bush of Ghosts*. And not only in Africa – I sensed these spirits everywhere else I went as well. Just like all of us, they long to be seen, to be noticed, to be loved. In broad daylight, when we are busy with ourselves, they tend to melt away. But come nightfall, they are part of the quiet topography we traverse, the wrinkle in our sheets, a fault line in our consciousness leading to moonlit hills in the distance. In these nightscapes, we sometimes transcend the distance to those hills, discovering places along the way which lie deep within ourselves.

Bon voyage!

National Youth

Remember when we came to this place?
Wilted flowers and bygone youth
Long on dreams so short on faith
So damned sure we knew the truth

Nowadays with each new dawn
The balding sun demands a price
Burning like August on a suburban lawn
Just one locust darkens the bluest skies

Accustomed to the axe, no strangers to wood
Friends hide away with their view of the seas
Strength in slumbers in these neighbourhoods
Where angry lions grace the mantelpiece

Hope fury then the fire of our imagination
Shedding warm light on the paths ahead
Trails were leaner, meaner, an alienation
Dead Sea scrolls yellowing the life we led

Nowadays it's better than we thought it was
Though each blessing carries its curse
On a placid sea, an eye on the albatross
Growing old sucks but the alternative is worse

Evaporate!

Watching water trickle
The cracks the crevices
The rain and melting ice
And snow making its way
Tiny pools, a rivulet, maybe a cupful
Splashed like fickleness of the heart
Borrowing the shape of its haven
Only long enough
To gather
Before a hot kiss of sunlight
In the funkhouse
Turns up the steam.

Vapour rises
Beads of moisture on your skin
Dancing all night with you
While I watch from the corner of my eye
Cold light, a winter moon rising
Wondering if its icy glare
Might freeze the water
Icy glitter
Dusting hearts and hands
While I plot the getaway
Robbing your day and mine
Of tired routines and rituals
Irrational hope germinates in my breast
An escape to a summer night's Shangri-La
Like water trickling
Between the old boards
Of a floor not really made for dancing.

Safe Keeping

Went to the bank brought them all my silver
They asked for more, they wanted my faith
Demanded my confidence in the future as well.

So what is it about them anyway?
Why does it feel like I was cheating them?
Perhaps I owed them more in return
For the paltry bit of interest they were feigning?

All I wanted on that day was to be with you.
In the open, not masquerading.
With an embrace as shelter and sanctuary
Against the storms which come and go
But never quite as strong as the bond
Two people find when there's no need
To hide your treasure
Or whatever else might be precious
From the prying eyes of others
Who will never understand
Why it isn't wise to keep your faith in the bank.

Where'd Ya Think I was Going?

Where'd ya think I was going
While you were out there chasing ghosts?
Trees was sighing, wind was blowing
The long road ended at the coast

Tell me stuff I don't wanna hear
Rain pounded me while I was tied to the post
Seasons passed me by, a whole damn year
T'was always nearly but never almost…

Where'd ya think I was going
While you were out there on the town
Nothing new nothing worth showing
Day was already done before the sun went down

Heard It Yesterday

Heard it on the YSP
You out there all jumpin' bad
Town's gone dark on you
All the jesters hopping mad

Land's awash feeling heady
Now's the time to push to sea
Forest coming down on you
No point hiding among the trees

Newsman warned me you were gone
Smiled his big-ass flatscreen grin
Mapped the route he said you'd choose
Not really knowing the state you're in

But I know you'll find the way
To the place you're meant to be
Twist and turn the whole way through
Dot my eyes then cross the tea

Back from LA

dream of the sun more often than we see it
in this place
so any kinda light might be a beacon of love
turn the corner whatever chance we get
and celebrate our nakedness

framed and caressed
the cool mad jumble of sheets
Whiteness awash in blinking big city neon
pinks and reds and yellows
pour in from outside the window

in the early hours
somber stripes of light and shadow
cast across your skin by the window blinds
a landscape resplendent
in salty sweaty dry smoothness

topographies trap-doors and magic mountains
above that fruited plain
wanton patterns of lingerie
tattooed on your back by the sand and sun
at the water's edge yesterday

push me pull me drive me
through the danger zone
like an eager mouth's excursions
for nourishment
a spot where city and countryside meet

sometimes i think being well-fed
doesn't mean as much as it used to
a promise redeemed at the drop of a hint
confusing curiosity with courage
and hunger with pain

Injustice Every Day

Said more than you knew
Heard more than just the news
Gave more than you had
Took more than they need

        In the end we all wonder
        Ain't enough to go around
        Sighing empty-handed
        Just what we wanted most

Let them blow your cover
Called them liars and lovers
Bit off more than they can chew
Bleeding pride in front of you

        Pain enough for one or two
        Lost it all when we looked away
        So careful with the bandages
        Those bandages in my head

Keep them all at bay
Hope they look the other way
Cried all night just for you
Cried more than just the blues...

Locked up tight no more keys
Draw the shades keep out the night
Shut your eyes to see the stars
When you squeeze out all the light

> So we sit and we wonder
> Why it's so fuckin' hot in here
> In the dark we sit and wonder
> Why we have to gasp for air

Keep them all at bay
Hope they look the other way
Cried all night just for you
Sure cried more than just the blues...

A Puppet Life

dangling on our strings
every time
the curtain rises
ventriloquists
lending us the voice we need

dreaming that we're free
but one tug
makes us miss our step
leave us tangled
up in the strings

not gonna take it anymore
we scream
ranting revolution in silent rage
eyes never blinking
minds never thinking

so rage and cut those strings
the ones that reign us in
we're lying helpless on the floor
beside the shiny scissors
which liberated us

spend our evenings tucked away
home in the drawer
puppeteer sings a merry tune
tying knots in the strings
that give us life

Autumn

Blew into town last night
In the dark
Like a leaf falling from a branch
High over your head
Teased by the wind of an autumn storm

Fell into the blackness
All around me
No summer moon to light the way
Rain and the wind lashing out
Impatiently erratically not angrily not spitefully

Tugged hard at the umbrella while I walked
Tiny needles of water in my face

Then standing next to you
Warm and radiant
Eyes iridescent like a night sky
Full of stars
So strong the wind didn't matter

All the raindrops I dodged
On the way
To a welcoming hearth in your embrace
Make the gardens grow
Bursting into bloom when I think of you

Futureworld

lazing on the shores of the mirror lake
my toes radiating in the breeze of chrome
we got cellular speakeasies we got protein breaks
we got custom-tailored chromosomes.

paradise she don't tell no lies
with her haunting fiber-optic eyes...

livestream skies matrixes and meadows
living our life in broadbands in the shadows
program's there to tell us we're happy
a cryogenic shame that the content's so crappy

guess it takes a while for the word to get around
with all the logic seems to be going on...

So Blue for Her

She rolls with the sea
She howls at the moon
She comes like the breeze
She tastes like June

The tempest inside
I breathe and I bleed
Dance in the night
Feet follow the beat

Her cards playing down
All those incidents
The boneyard's craving
Some kinda accident

Run for it now
While the coast is clear
Kissing her hard now
While she's breaking here

The boneyard's torment's
All about love and the heat
With two rolled into one
You gotta feel the beat

We just say so...
We just say so...

Blues from a Bottle

Spied me while you crawled in the fog
Outside the door to the saloon
Said you were out walking the dog
Down on the floor howling at the moon
Laying tracks help ya find the way back
A trick a treat, those liquor tricks you cravin' for

Run out of things to say after a while I guess
Drew a blank when your name came up
Dark and slippery slopes, give you more for less
Squeezin' the juice trying to drain the cup
You're laying back looking for the tracks
Work up a sweat doing those liquor tricks you slavin' for

Suffocating dark all stuffy and far away
Air's thick and white and hot as cotton
Things don't feel quite right today
Never noticed how much you'd forgotten
Bottle on the board, dead in those tracks trying to get back
Break your ass doing those liquor tricks you cravin' for

Bonefish Boogie

Breezing in the wilderness
Walking on the wind
And a solstice of sorts

Head's full of ideas
Images hanging in the air
Feeding that badass buzz

Funky lady knows the lines
Bravely bold and spend the time
Touching on her badass buzz

No hungry beasts to dodge upstream
Spawning light the air we breath
Sharing life and the love we need

City Girl

got words about her ways
up and down the walls
all around the corners
pulsing to the beat of a neon sign
in the shop window
selling aspirations.

Summer symphony skirts and skin
Dancing like some sunshine sparkles
tinsel diamonds on the street
flowing like the pavement
beneath my feet

lacking pedal digits she laughs
whispering to me
toeless is what she means
rooted to the ground like cornstalks
whose ears listen for the sound

of movement
of motion

Coming Up for Air

Screaming you can't breathe
any air that isn't free
a few of us having parties
gotta be the one for you and me.
you already got a party?
so we see...

do a wing-ding for ole Joe you know
without whom, well, where'd we be?
don't be no ass 'cos he's our man
he's hip
he's sure not Stalin
he shoo-be-doo ain't no Tito
he's the real McCarthy...

got secrets make you gasp
chokin' on Hollywood Hoboken 1950?
players change, not the acts
don't twist no arms, just twist some facts
dogs down every alley
barking up every tree.

So boy, you'd better stop turning blue
when we talk to you ...

In December

Icy cold where I slept
Dreaming of the sun
Awake at your side
Smell of your skin
Your hair tickling my cheek
Rhythm of your breath reminds me of the beach.

I lay awake this morning
Gazing over your shoulder
And beyond
Out the window
Frost on the branches outside
A cap of snow on the bird's nest.

Later in the afternoon
When it got dark
Cinnamon and cloves saturate the air.
Hot fruit and berries
Spices by your side
And anise dotting the heavens like stars.

Winter darkness hiding
Opportunities we have missed
Stars as tiny pinpoints
Light the way where warmth makes winter bearable
Where untold mysteries lay
With springtime just around the corner.

Electrify Me

Driving me hard like your Tesla, Baby
Driving me all insane...
Drive me bed me floor me, Baby
Drive me all insane...

Spark my plugs and charge me, Baby
Driving me all insane...
Juice me with that power port, Baby
Just drive me all insane...

Making miles with you all night, Baby
Drives me all insane...

Hundred Years

Hundred years
Lotta tears
Lotta beers
All those years

Living in arrears
Haunted by fears
Taunted by peers
All those years

Shopping at Sears
Calling me queer
Dropping outta gear
Stopping by to leer

Had my ear so long
For some hundred years goin' strong
Sky's gotta clear this much I know
But you won't be here shoveling snow

Hundred years
Lotta tears

Empty Houses

never forget your smile
how fiercely that cold wind blew
on that November day
i learned the truth
about you and that barren Spanish ground
at Mejadora del Campo.

There's a song in my heart
for you
about you and
Madrid and
empty houses and me
back in 1983.

Falling Angels

Drag me out behind your shed
Flog me with your treasures till I'm good and dead
Knocking the habeus corpus outta my head
And then you're gonna mourn
All woe and lament
Asking where the hell
Your civilization went

Meeting me back there behind the bushes
But cowering when your pleasure flushes red
Sucking up your ego all luscious
And the righteous raise their voices in scorn
You'll dance and sing
While the angels try to figure out
Why they let you clip their wings

Summer

Fireflies dotting
An inky blackness outside the window
Like a celestial tapestry
We celebrated our nakedness
A mouth following the contour of your breast
The tip of a tongue
Hiding mischievously
In the stubblefield
Between your legs.

Maybe I was only dreaming
But I thought
You came in more flavors
Than the Baskin Robbins store
Down the road,
That cathedral of bright lights and vanilla and candy
Whose cold but silent glare
Held the fireflies at bay
While I slept in the warmth of your body
At home
At last
In your arms.

Nighttime in America

racing thru the arteries of the city
like corpuscles in our veins
air's hot the breath of a dog all warm
and humid and smelly fetid ozone Purina
car lots rolling by our window
lights flags and stars all dazzling and radiant overhead
steal our sense of direction
lost in the music the radio blares a beat to beat back the heat...

sharing love and food and life and time i give you mine
no gifts hidden in a motherfunkylode gotta play today
cos it won't stay the day you step into the bright light
body naked cold your soul a featherweight on the wind
while everybody 'round you mourning
with their shovels in hand how quick the time be passing
all the time we wasted just tryin' to beat back the heat...

be warm skin naked free when there's water in the well
just step up to the jam cos in a dry spell
when the door falls shut we be wasting our breath
asking desperados to show us the way back to where we left our keys
so we know where to look when we think we've found the lock
that keeps us in a cage and safe from diversion
thinking it's the place we could retreat to to beat back the heat...

when i stop walking talking at the water's edge
can't go no further no drinking the sludge in our cup
it's only saltwater like tears and sweat or jellyfish
far as the eye can see
no one out here i'm thirsty as hell
catch me when i fall no one hears my call
i'm tired as hell stay up all night chasing ghosts distraction
so that i don't see the empty pillow where you sleep
when i'm dreaming of you
my stomach growls i'm hungry
while my heart beats a meaner beat to beat back the heat...

Plenty of Reasons

Plenty of reasons to cry in the night
Plenty of reasons to put up a fight
Plenty of reasons to push back the tide
Plenty of reasons to sharpen the knives
Plenty of reasons to get on with our lives...

Plenty of reasons to get back on the road
Plenty of reasons to lighten my load
Plenty of reasons to kiss an ugly toad
Plenty of reasons to get our cuts sewed
Plenty of reasons to collect the debts you're owed...

Made a break floored it today hustling all alone blasting a trail through the fast lane
Skid marks gone all washed away sliding in the endzone 'cos you couldn't stop the rain

Plenty of reason for rags to riches
Plenty of reasons to count the stitches
Plenty of reasons to make the switches
Plenty of reasons to hit the ditches
Plenty of reasons to curve the pitches...

Wanna Know Why

Wanna know why
Hadda be this way
Wanna know why
Hadda be today

House was steaming hot
Sweat running down my face
You and me's getting hot
Flowers wilting in the vase

Hadda come to this place
Hadda run this race
Hadda pray for saving grace
Didn't wanna lose no face

The projects spit out their sons
Told me we were going down
Small minds scared in a great big world
Making us learn the hard way
Dropping dead in the name of fun
Lotta that kinda stuff going down
Breathing easy while poison flags unfurled
After a real hard day

So I wanna know why
Hadda be this way

The It's-All-in-God's-Hands Blues

me had a vision
looking through the walls of a house
where sinners spinners winners bide their time.

they work machines and push the clocks
they turn the stars they mark our time.
say they know when you're gonna rise
who you're gonna be who you're gonna leave behind.

'cause you sold them your trust the day they said
their god was gonna make things easy for you
they knew they're gonna do a deal with you
and there's only one small thing that you have to do ...

you break your butt you break your back
and all they promise is to wake you when it's over
and all you need to do is give 'em your trust
when they say things gonna work out for you.

you see that house got barbed wire round the altar
keep people like us from stealing the lord's treasure

or maybe just his wisdom
so while you're waiting for that shoe to drop
they're gonna wanna call, make a deal with you.

they work machines they push the clock
they turn the stars they mark the time.

Hotspot

Homin' in on that hotspot baby
Lemme ride yer wave
Heads up between the swells now baby
Surfing surging
Those five long laps to your treasure

Icon blinking when I think of you baby
Hailing the mighty provider
Homin' in on your hotspot honey
Riding the rough
In five full bars of signal pleasure

Swipe your screen
Build up some steam
Swipe your screen
It's like a dream

Rainy Days

Woke up this morning
sun wouldn't shine
rained all day
sun didn't shine

sold all my things
took the long way home
packed all my things
took the long way home

my baby left this morning
didn't say goodbye
my baby she gone this morning
she didn't say why

cooked me some coffee
lord, she didn't even say why
sippin' on my coffee
guess i'm gonna die

angels be calling
leading me home
wet ground's a-calling
calling me home

saying don't you forget
those old hollow bones
No don't you forget
your old soggy bones

An Invitation

Invited me to the exhibition
Standing side-by-side
Lifetime of lampshades lining the wall

So there I stood
Hovering next to you,
Blood sweat and tears on a canvas looked like me

So sure that I could read
The writing between the lines
Whitewashed mortar primary colours hanging mute

Stepped out the door
Looked up saw the rainbow
Dripping the same saturated colours you breathe

I recognized you then
Finally dawned why you invited me
A dry brush and me like the old master you were seeing

Living your Lies

Tired of that pious poverty
You wearin' like a badge
Like a ticket getcha past Heaven's gate
Worked so hard give you hope and work
Worked so damn hard not to give up hope

Gave you all the knowledge you lost
When you veered away from your horizon
Scared the sea was full of serpents
Dropping from the trees in your garden
Back then when the world was flat

And now it's a wasteland, so flat again
And the line where sea and sky embrace
A threshold of pain and fear
You're convinced your brother can't cross
Confusing a chip on your shoulder
With a book holding all the faith a man can carry

Don't need to learn no more
'cos your hands are deep in blood
Red from ripping at your brother's heart
Red from raping the women who would love you
Longing for a past that will never shine
Because its light is only redeemable
At the edge of an open grave

Online Tonight

Thoroughly modern me
Waxing and waning
Relishing my connectivity
Can't fall for you
Got other things to do...

Got a life like a casting show
Busy managing my likes
So damn much choice don't know where to go
But I can't fall for you
'cos I got better things to do...

Swipe me tender little bitch
Let me know that I'm the one
Swipe the icons making my touchscreen itch
But I won't fall for you
'cos I got other things to do...

Thoroughly cool this modern me
Waxing Brazilian all alone
And cut the light 'cos I'm relishing my connectivity

Rambling with My Rohrschachs

It's circus out there steals me from my sleep
Turning night-time into day

Mining daydreams way down in your deep
Taunting our ghosts along the way

Eyes wide open worship the company I keep
The things we do our best not to say

We're carnival a gang of clowns that weep
When the clouds of confetti blow away

...and we the people be like those tiny water droplets make up the cumulus clouds and the fog billowing up like some big massive bubbling body that can only keep its shape as long as the water droplets never ever touch each other 'cos when they do then they drop like rocks and ice from the sky like rain on a dark and stormy day a downpour that runs like rivulets across your face tumbling to the ground and running into the gutters at the side of the street escaping into the darkness of an underworld of pipes and sewage where even the thought of touching is an act of revulsion and rebellion and everyone pools their aspirations dreaming of being a part of a fluffy white cloud high up there in the sky...

Other times other places you're out there
Running other races
Other times other places you're out there
Seeking different faces
Turning night-time into day...

Things You Do!

Dream in blue
Solitary shoe
A wider view
Seams showing through beneath your déjà vu

Making tons of hay
Giving night and day
The united way
Clippings thrown away intentions gone astray

Things you do
Remind me of you...
High on pride
A beachfront bride in a wanton tide

Hearts abound in subdivision
Kisses linger like long division
Mono-channel television
Cold fire in the kitchen cuts with clean precision

Things you do
Make me feel for you....
Cold draft through the room
Madman in groom in his hand's an iron broom

Things you do
Remind me of you...
Break my heart in two
Make me fight for you make me wiggle through

When the Americans Came

Balls-to-the-wall and free-for-all
Riding tall to the shopping mall
Deep stall balls to the wall

Say we traded our treasure for a handful of silver

Spent it trumping chumps at the local dumps
Avoid the bumps taking our lumps
While they trumped that chump at the local dump

And when the Americans came
Finally slew the jackboot dragons
Everyone jumping onto the wagon
Forgetting that the garbage in their soul's
The price they pay for the blood on their hands
In the days before the Americans came

Now we want them to remember us in their prayers
Wanna see them in church every goddamn day
But we only go there for the buzz and for the wine
Fondly romancing a wicked past
Grown pristine with the passage of time
After the Americans came

Riding the Bus

Back seat in the bus
Tune of wheels humming on the road
While I'm making my way to you

Half of humanity's crowded
Behind a row of tinted glass
Smile every mile I come closer to you

Street out there is like your skin
Every curve takes me where I wanna be
Every turn a surprise see the lights in your eyes

Anywhere and everywhere will do
And every corner the Greyhound lets me off
A nicer place because it brings me closer to you

The Waiting Game

Trying to stay sane, brain's a sponge mop
Showering blame like petals in a flower shop
Playing games with you on top
Waiting for the shoe to drop
Waiting for the rain to stop…

Big swigs making me a party to my own revival
Swinging through like the small-town carnival
Patience ain't a virtue, it's about survival
This town's been longing for a festival
But I'm just waiting for your arrival

Dodging ticker-tape raining through the air
Land at home with nothing to declare
Papering over some hurting love affair
Keeping your eyes open for a new concessionaire
Glimpse over your shoulder some quiet despair

So tell me this
Your beautiful kiss
Is it bliss?
Or an abyss?
Are there even two of us in this?

Spring and July

Me and you Baby on the road
Highway silver skyway gold
Electric touching steady hand
Chasing down some promised land

Chestnuts cars and whippoorwills
No shining stars no dollar bills
Moonrock moonwalk smell of clover
Scratch my back and roll me over

We're driving slow living fast
Wondering how it's gonna last
Soft shoe shuffles tread on air
Fingers on fire in my hair

But did Bloody Mary's heart go red
Is your magic really dead?
Feels that way the whole way back
When the road go rocky sky go black.

Taxi Blues

Meter's flagged nowhere to go
Tears in my eyes, just don't know
Where the road ahead lies
Where the time flies
When I wasn't looking

Cryin'...
Cryin' in the back seat of a taxi
Ain't it so strange
How I run outta change
I can't pay the fare
No one wants to drive me there
'cos the road's too far
A mile at most to where you are
But it's all too damned far

Since you've gone away for good

Sunset

Loitering under an iron sky
Marvel at the bands of silver
Rivers run between the mountains
Twisting turning to the sea.
Bridges straddle the flow in silence
The sound of rushing gurgling water
Permeates the air around us

How to fool yourself make a fantasy feel real
Dreaming of that moment
You wrap your arms around it
Catching up with your hopes and wishes
While you run as fast as you can
Mistaking the breeze in your face for the feeling you recall
The time you sailed across a stormy sea
Looking for refuge in a harbour which felt like home
If someone hadn't roused you
From your slumber

Watching as your dreams fade away
Audacious and delicious as they were that day
Sinking like the sun behind an ocean
Reflected in pupils of Bonaparte's eyes
On his faraway island
Where his dreams were swallowed by a green forest
Creeping up from behind while he squinted
Unaware that he was looking
In the wrong direction.

Wanna be a Fan of Miley's

bag-in and shagging it
the irony of it all
and that iron ball bit
when she shows it all

adrenalining us flash her brawns and brains
leaves her boys all wrapped in chains
i wanna take the time and cruise thru Vegas
ring her chimes and maybe buy a Degas

she's swinging by
she's getting high
setting her nashville precendent
but surely not by accident
she don't need to be so abstinent

so like me thru association please
socialmeteorized and guaranteed
a million tiny screens all bright at night
banging on the door wanna come inside

The Wind in your Face

Waiting on the day she promises to stay
Wasting away till the breeze blows your way
Kisses and wishes
Kisses and wishes...

Stars in your eyes just like the evening sky
Trust in her style just don't ask her why
Wishes and kisses
Wishes and kisses...

Reason's cast away you're caught in her sway
Like a castaway waiting for the break of day
Kisses and wishes
Kisses and wishes...

A script to write 'cos her love is burning bright
Fleeing from the night in her fancy you'll take flight
Wishes and kisses
Wishes and kisses...

Feet on the ground glad at what you've found
Four and twenty blackbirds with her all around

Yer Beauty Mark

Yer beauty mark's got gravity all its own
Spinning me 'round and 'round
Like some falling star
Blazing when I touch your atmosphere

Yer beauty mark's got gravity all right
Got me racing 'round in your orbit
Like some radiant Kahoutek thing
Lighting me up in your atmosphere

That beauty mark's got me tied in knots
Fueling the fusion the fire inside
Like a moth heading to the flame
Burning bright when I touch your atmosphere

Lantern

Ran as hard as I could
Far as my feet gonna carry me
From that spot
Where I'd pulled up the roots
Trying to plant a seed.

Afraid to go back because I'd run so far
Afraid to go forth because I'd not run far enough
Gasping
I was out of breath
Scared of losing sight of where I'd been
Not knowing what lies ahead
In your hand I saw a light
Held way up high
But not the beacon I hoped it might be
Because I wasn't sure
If you were lighting the way
As you emerged from the darkness
In retreat
From the blackness still shrouding
The path that lay ahead of me.

In the Ocean

If I could reach out far enough
Hold my breath long enough
All the way to the other side
Where you
Stand at the opposite shore looking
With the same sense of yearning

Sometimes the calm of your surface
Belies the turmoil beneath
While at other times the turmoil on your surface
Belies the calm below
Where I would float in a weightless world
Of silence and broken light

In the dense atmosphere of your deep
Starfish constellations
Creeping across their sandy firmament
Mirroring the heavens high over my head
Hidden from the view of a terrestrial world
That holds me in gentle captivity
Far removed
From your watery spell

Sleepless I think of you
As I roll restlessly in my sleep
Just as the ocean does
In its bed at night

The Visit

Felt pretty strange visiting
The city where I fell in love with you
All by myself
It was warm sun was shining
Just like it always did when you were here
How good it felt to breathe the air
Charged with that special electricity
Erasing the boundaries
Where my life bordered upon yours
Sharing laughs and drinks and food
And the gift of time

It's all different nowadays
Still a big stage of people parades
Of drama and comedies
Celebration and fantasies
But I'm alone in the audience.
So while I now have my choice of seating
The only show worth watching
Is for those who walk and dance in their sleep
Watching mutely as old papers blow through dark
And empty streets
And when the dream is over
And the traffic finally grinds to a halt
I awake to find that you've gone away.

Tricked Me into Thinking

Tricked me into thinking
I was in love with you

Spent my days digging a hole
Like some goddamn mole
Burrowing its way to the light
Scratch and claw and maul and bite
On our own
That's sure no way to knead the clay

Contessa out selling me them skin patches
Make me invisible when the crowd's a-trippin'
Shield them from my sight with my magic glove
Me all naked
Losing my shape, my colour and my sleight of hand

Why don'tcha move
Together with me?
And stop tricking me into thinking
I was in love with you

Weekend Wager

People more knowledgeable than I
Warn me often to watch my head.
To be wary of a sky
Where the strong winds of change
Blow with the seductive scent of flowers.
Cautioning me to hedge my bets
Not to overstep the lines and borders
Where wild blossoms threaten to spill over
The fences around my heart
Upsetting their gardener's sense of order.

"I've never been a gambling man!" I tell them

Pleased their reason is so compelling
They pound me on the back
Impressing upon me the need to heed
The wisdom which they're selling.
But I'm smiling as I turn to go
No need to make them understand
That I've already taken my chances
Just by loving you.

You Told Me

You told me we needed to go
You told me we needed to know
You told me we had nothing to show
Despite all the gains…

You told me we better pray
You told me gonna waste away
You told me gonna have to pay
For all our pains…

You told me we better swim
You told me the odds are slim
You told me the light's going dim
Holding the reigns…

You told me things are gonna be wild
You told me I'd cry like a child
You told me you saw me smile
At the noise we make when we rattle our chains

Intercity

all those greyhaired men
in dark trench coats
stand silently
wordless
no face behind their expressions
in deep canyons of shadow
fog-shrouded train stations
as the night express carries me home.

am I carrying any secrets tonight?

that string of lights that rush past
the coach windows
at irregular intervals
under the solemn cover of the night
hide the faces
of those
that stand
watching from the darkness beyond.

life without parole
or parole without life?
forever is such a long time to spend alone
with you on my mind